"As someone who, through the grace of God, rebuild a marriage, I can say that this book struggling. First and foremost, it helps hus definition of marriage as God ordained it. Se doable action items for everyday people with busy effort to apply the advice in *101 Tips for a Happier Marriage*, their relationship only with their spouse but also with the Lord—will be the best it can be."

Teresa Tomeo
Host of *Catholic Connection*

"How can something as wide and complex as marital conflict be addressed by a book so slender and simple? Our culture stresses the wedding day and forgets the married life—until the wheels start coming off and then it's often too late. But there is hope. This wise and practical book is not only for couples who want to make their good marriages great, but is even better for couples who, for their own unique and pain-drenched reasons, find themselves tempted to give up on the dream. To Dr. Jennifer Roback Morse and Betsy Kerekes go the laurels for this much-needed manual for strengthening men and women for what G. K. Chesterton called the 'duel to the death which no man of honor should decline.'"

Patrick Coffin
Host of *Catholic Answers Live*

"This is the best assimilation of received and gathered wisdom on marriage I've seen. In short and pithy darts of advice, the authors deliver universal truths in sharp and witty zingers that are at times brilliant revelations and bracing reminders of what we 'can't not know,' but somehow keep forgetting. This book is for every couple preparing for the sacrament and every couple holding up the institution through thick and thin. Bold and practical, this gem is a gift and a guide for everyone in all stages of life. I love it!"

Sheila Liaugminas
Host of *A Closer Look*

"*101 Tips for a Happier Marriage* is full of practical, helpful ideas to keep a marriage alive and well. It should be handed out to every couple going through a pre-Cana program. If every couple followed its advice, there would be many more happy and successful marriages!"

Patrice Fagnant-MacArthur
Author of *The Catholic Baby Name Book*

"At last! A good and reliable guide to what it takes to make a marriage work and make it last a lifetime. The authors show us that a successful marriage is more about being good than feeling good. Being a good spouse is about being a good person.

Virtue is the key to a happy marriage as it is the key to a happy life. If love is about laying down our life for our friends, marriage is about laying down our life for our best friend. This little gem of a book should be read by every married couple and by those planning to get married."

Joseph Pearce
Author of *The Quest for Shakespeare*

"The Morse-Kerekes approach to making marriage last is a solid, frank presentation of the major issues that come up or can come up in any marriage. In addition, in the anti-marriage climate of our time, the authors face frankly the arguments given for deviant or alternative ways and directly point out why such views are erroneous. This is a very fundamental approach by writers who know in-depth what is at issue for families, Church, and society."

James V. Schall, S.J.
Professor of Political Philosophy
Georgetown University

"Finally, a book that combines a deep understanding of the truth of marriage with essential advice about how to make marriage work. Reading this book will make you a better spouse because it will make you a better person. I will be giving *101 Tips for a Happier Marriage* to every new couple I know."

Angela Franks
Theological Institute for the New Evangelization
St. John's Seminary

"An eye-opening, energizing, attitude-adjusting, wake-up-call-of-a-book that every married couple should read and re-read. A power-packed energy drink of marital wisdom and truth."

Tom Allen
Founding Editor and President of *Catholic Exchange*

"Marriage is a sacrament—holy and profound in meaning. But to the person wondering how he or she can continue to live with the stranger on the other side of the bed, the theology of marriage seems a distant abstraction. When the mechanics of a marriage—communication, respect, affection—are broken, a lecture on the theoretical physics of it is of limited value. What you want is a practical toolbox: the words, the gestures, and small everyday acts that can get it running again. This is exactly what is provided in this little treasure of a book. Do this, not that. Say this, not that. Even: think this, not that. Whether your marriage needs only a little tune-up, or a major overhaul, *101 Tips for a Happier Marriage* is essential reading."

Mary Kochan
Editor-in-Chief of *Catholic Lane*

101 TIPS for a HAPPIER MARRIAGE

Simple Ways for Couples to Grow Closer to God and to Each Other

JENNIFER ROBACK MORSE & BETSY KEREKES
of The Ruth Institute

ave maria press AMP Notre Dame, Indiana

Founded in 1865, Ave Maria Press is a ministry of the United States Province of Holy Cross.

www.avemariapress.com

Paperback: ISBN-10 1-59471-466-0, ISBN-13 978-1-59471-446-7

E-book: ISBN-10 1-59471-447-9, ISBN-13 978-1-59471-447-4

Cover image © Thinkstock.com

Cover and text design by Brian C. Conley.

Printed and bound in the United States of America.

Library of Congress Cataloging-in-Publication Data is available.

God is God.

You are not.

Your spouse is not.

Contents

ACKNOWLEDGMENTS

We are both grateful to the staff and supporters of the Ruth Institute. This project began before the Ruth Institute existed, but the Ruth Institute staff made this a better book, and Ruth Institute readers blessed us with their feedback.

Jennifer
The book you are holding in your hand is a project of many loves in my life. Love for my husband, first of all. Love for my children, for whom our marriage was so important. Love for my readers, and finally, love for my friend and coauthor, Betsy Kerekes.

Betsy

For this book being made possible, I'd like to thank the following people: First and foremost, our Heavenly Father, without whom this book, my marriage, my faith, and my life would not exist. I owe it all to you. Secondly, I thank my coauthor, Jennifer Morse, for allowing me to collaborate with you. It's been an honor. Next is my beloved husband Paul. Thanks for being so wonderful at this whole marriage thing and for giving me perspective on how a happy marriage looks! And finally, the people at Ave Maria Press, starting with a seemingly chance encounter with Dianna Leinen, leading me to Kristi McDonald and the rest of the AMP staff. Thank you for all that you do.

INTRODUCTION

WHY YOU WANT THIS BOOK

Every person who gets married in the Catholic Church today is making some pretty bold statements:

- Almighty God wants me to love my spouse for the rest of my life.
- I am making a commitment to love this person, even if he or she becomes difficult.
- Even if my spouse becomes nearly impossible to live with, I will continue to act in an attitude of love toward him or her.

- Loving my spouse is part of my personal path to holiness.

Like I said, pretty bold statements.

Considering the ease of divorce in the event of problems, the ease of cohabitation as a substitute for marriage, and the frequency of women choosing to become unmarried mothers, entering into a sacramental marriage is, at the very least, countercultural. Marriage is no longer the socially expected, normal life path that people coast along on auto-pilot. Marriage is an adventure in cultural renewal, an adventure in self-consciously building up what Blessed John Paul II called "a civilization of love."

The book you are holding in your hand is designed to help you live up to these bold commitments. Perhaps you want a better marriage for yourself or someone you love. Maybe you are about to get married and want to start off on the right foot. Or maybe you have young friends who are about to marry and you want to support them. Maybe you have a friend whose marriage is in trouble. Maybe you are frustrated with your spouse.

So why this book, rather than all the many others out there? This book empowers you. You do not have to wait for the other person to go to therapy, get an attitude change, or anything else. You can have a better marriage starting right now. You can take steps today that will bring you closer to God and His plan for you, and for your marriage.

But why should you want a better marriage? Why not just coast along with a "settle-for" marriage? Why not join the parade and get divorced? Because deep down, you believe in the power of love. You want to learn more about what spousal love is and how to love rather than give yourself an exit option.

Spousal love for the sake of the married couple: The family is the first school of love. The family is where men and women learn to overcome their disagreements and bring their complementary differences together in a unified whole. Our recent popes, John Paul II and Benedict XVI, have both expressed thoughts along these lines, many times.

Spousal love for the sake of the children: The family is where children learn to love and be loved. The parents' love for one another is the greatest gift they can give to their children. The stability and loving-ness of the parents' union is the foundation for their children's entire lives. Children whose parents re-mained married in a low-conflict union throughout their childhoods have the best life chances. Chil-dren of divorced or never-married parents are at risk for a whole variety of problems, including a reluctance to trust and to form marriages of their own.

Spousal love for the sake of society: When marriages break down or fail to form, the entire society suf-fers. Children deprived of parental love and guid-ance have a way of creating problems for others. Adults who are playing the field at an age when they should be settled in love can create instabili-ty around them. Taxpayers end up footing the bill for expensive services that try to take the place of absent or preoccupied parents. And every person who has been disappointed in love is a sitting duck for all kinds of alleged substitutes for the family, whether taxpayer-supported programs, "alternative lifestyles," or religious heresies.

We become mistrustful of anyone who claims to love us, even God Himself. In our loneliness and lovelessness, we may become vulnerable to people who claim to minister to us, but who may not have our best interests at heart. In our woundedness, we may become suspicious of those who really do want to help us and do have our best interests at heart.

Having a happy marriage matters to a lot more people than just the two of you. And a happy and successful marriage is about more than you and your feelings. It is far better to work with the marriage you have rather than to keep trying to switch out the partners, hoping for a better deal.

What This Book Is Not

This book is not therapy or medical support. In other words, this book is *not* for people with addiction issues or domestic violence issues. Addictions today, sadly, can include much more than drugs and alcohol. Increasingly, sex and pornography addictions are becoming huge barriers to marital happiness. If you believe you or your spouse has any addiction issues, I beg you to seek more help than you can get from a little book like this one. You may need medical support, therapeutic help, a self-help group, spiritual advice, or legal counsel.

If you are dealing with domestic violence in your marriage, you must also seek assistance. No book is enough to help you discern what to do in that extreme situation. You may need to live separately from your spouse, for your own safety and the safety of your children.

In all such cases, I would urge you to confide in a spiritual director or your pastor. You want to be sure that you are living in accordance with the will of God and if you're Catholic, the teachings of the Catholic Church.

Except for these dire circumstances, my statement stands: You are better off working with the marriage you have, with the partner you have, than trying to switch around partners.

Because you see, one of the biggest barriers to your own happiness is certainly you! You will be part of any other relationship you get into. If you decide to live alone, you will be living with yourself. You might as well learn some of these important strategies for better relationships now rather than later.

A Word about How to Use This Book

Don't leave this book around for your spouse to find. I'm not kidding. This book is for *you*. The whole point of the book is that *you* can improve your marriage, even if your spouse doesn't change a bit. I advocate that people speak as clearly as they can about what they think, want, and need. Dropping hints and leaving stuff lying around can be manipulative. Either speak up, if you want something from your spouse, or work the tips yourself, without necessarily telling your spouse what you are doing.

Someone has to take the first steps in love. Someone has to be the first to let go of old resentments. Someone has to be the first to forgive. Someone has to give the first compliment or express the first gratitude. It needs to be you. Why? Because you have this book in your hand. Because you care.

Last, have some fun. Loving your spouse is your unique key to heaven. Our Lord wants us to be joyful, even when the path seems difficult. Your efforts to find and create joy in your family will pay for themselves many times over, even if your spouse doesn't change a bit.

One last observation: Both of us are Roman Catholics, and our publisher is a Catholic publisher. Everything in this book is consistent with Catholic teaching. Because the truths taught by the Catholic Church on marriage and family are held by many faiths, most of what is in this book will be perfectly compatible with most forms of Christianity and Judaism. You can give this book to your friends in mixed marriages or friends from other Christian churches. They, too, will find it very helpful.

So, enjoy the adventure of building a better marriage for yourself, your family, and your community. And we'll see you in heaven, if not sooner!

MAKE A
DECISION TO LOVE

Love is a decision, not just a feeling.

1

Think about what is in your spouse's interest. A loving person wants the best for another and is willing to follow through with actions.

Many disappointments in married life can be traced to one basic misunderstanding: we think love is a feeling. We think we are "in love" when we like the way we feel with the other person. But timeless wisdom shows that love is more than a feeling. Love is a decision. You can improve your marriage by making a decision to love. In fact, you can improve the lives of many people by making the decision to do what is in their interest, even if it is inconvenient for you at the time.

2

Help your spouse grow by being the first to step outside the comfort zone.

It is easy to be tempted to hold ourselves back from emotional and spiritual growth because we are afraid that our new selves will not be accepted by our spouse. Fear is never a good excuse to refrain from growing closer to God or each other. Make a leap of courage by pushing yourself emotionally and spiritually, and hope that your spouse will be inspired by your actions. Be patient with yourself and your spouse.

3

Remain in solidarity with the other person, especially when he or she is suffering or struggling. Love sits by the bedside, even when it is painful to watch.

An easy way to show support for your spouse is to be present and available to them when they are going through a challenging time. It might be frustrating to listen to your spouse complain, or it might be sad for you to watch your loved one in pain, but your silent presence will communicate to both of you your commitment to your relationship.

4

Allow yourself to be surprised by joy. A loving person knows that he or she does not know everything and is willing to learn more about the other person. Your partner undoubtedly has many wonderful qualities you have not yet discovered.

Here's a great excuse for a date night: Why not go to dinner and try to come up with stories you have not yet told each other? Start by thinking of your earliest memory and working your way up from there. Make a game of it! It could be lots of fun, and you'll likely learn a great deal more about each other.

In the true story, *A Severe Mercy*, Sheldon Vanauken and his wife wanted so much to know and experience everything the other had ever done that they made a point to read every book the other had ever read. Now that's devotion. And you can have it too.

5

Enjoy the warm fuzzy feelings, but don't feel cheated if they go away. Feelings are fleeting. "I like the way I feel with this person" is not enough to sustain a marriage for a lifetime.

People often get divorced because they simply fall out of love with each other. "The chemistry is gone," they say. It's impossible to stay madly in love 24/7, but it is possible to keep a fire going that rivals the Olympic torch. Simple reminders of your feelings for each other (past and present) can help keep the flame alive. Read old journals from when you first met. Leave love notes for each other. Make up a scavenger hunt with a romantic prize at the end. The possibilities are endless, and falling in love with the same person can be just as exhilarating the second, third, and twelfth time around.

6

Expect to have variations in your level of sexual desire. Love is not the same as lust.

If you really want to rekindle that spark, practice natural family planning. Nothing makes you want your spouse more than abstaining for a period of time. And once that abstinence time is over, the sparks will fly—in a good way!

ADJUST
YOUR ATTITUDE

Change your thinking and be happier.

7

Remember that only God is God. Let your spouse be human. Give your spouse a break from always being perfectly understanding, always loving, and always there for you.

Ask yourself this: Are you always perfectly understanding, loving, and there for your spouse? It's highly unlikely that you are, and if you're not perfect, then how can you expect your spouse to be? Only God is perfect. Let God be your example and your guide.

8

Accept the fact that you are limited, imperfect, and fallible. You do not have to control everything in the world around you. Realize that you are not God.

Married couples must understand that they are not all-powerful. Stuff happens. You will be tried and tested. Remember to pray. Don't fall apart. Deal with it the best you can. Then move on.

9

Concentrate on changing yourself, which you have the power to do. Leave your spouse some room for his or her own growth process.

The expression "You can't change a person" is often used, and with good reason. People have to be willing to change their ways. That desire has to come from within, not from you. You can nudge and nag all you want, but that may only cause resentment and resistance. Instead, take a closer look at yourself. While it is humanly impossible to be perfect, you can still do your best. Ask yourself: What about myself could use improvement for the betterment of my marriage? Consider changing your reactions to the imperfections of your spouse. It's possible that he or she has just as much to put up with as you do.

10

Take responsibility for your own happiness. Your spouse does not really have the power to make you happy or miserable. You have a choice about how to react to what your spouse succeeds or fails to do.

If there is one thing you can control in your relationship, it's how you react to the things that happen around you. Try planning your reactions in your head by imagining future (potentially irritating) conversations with your spouse. Practice graceful responses like, "I'm sorry that you feel that way. What can we do to make you feel like I'm on your side right now?"

11

Take responsibility for meeting your own needs. You can take care of yourself. Know that you will survive, no matter what your spouse chooses to do or not do.

Knock yourself out of the mindset that your spouse has often done this or that for you, and therefore should *always* do those things for you. Sometimes that just won't be possible, and that's okay, because you're a big kid. You will survive, even if it means squishing the big spider yourself, pulling the chair over to reach the top shelf on your own, or cooking for yourself. It may mean listening to "Eye of the Tiger" several times in advance, but you can do it.

12 _____

Make a decision to take care of household issues that really matter to you. You won't need to nag your spouse about something truly important to you because you will be solving the problem yourself.

Believe it or not, social scientists have studied the question of housework: who does it, who complains about it, and what difference it makes. Study after study shows that women are happier when they feel appreciated for their contributions, and men are happier when they don't feel nagged. So, if the housework is nagging at you, don't nag at each other! Just take care of it! And if your spouse takes care of something, say thank you.

13

Make a decision to let go of the small stuff. If it isn't important enough for you to take care of yourself, it isn't important enough to nag your spouse about.

You really think the kitchen garbage can needs to be scrubbed out. Your spouse disagrees. You may be right. But you may have to accept the fact that you're going to be scrubbing it yourself. Or you may need to just let it go for a couple days longer than you originally hoped. Until you need to call the Health Department, letting it go is perfectly fine.

14

Be grateful for the good things in your life. Avoid feeling sorry for yourself at all costs. Self-pity is deadly because it drains the joy out of your life.

It's impossible to go through life and have everything go your way all the time. Sometimes bad stuff happens, and sometimes really bad stuff happens. Remember that no matter how terrible things may seem, there is always someone who has it worse. When you think things are rough for you, ponder the Passion of Christ and gain some perspective. Then rely on the Lord to help you.

15

Let the differences between you and your spouse become a source of strength. It is a scientifically proven fact that men and women differ in significant ways. Appreciate and use these differences, rather than fight over them.

It's okay that he normally takes out the trash and she normally washes the dishes. Don't fret about falling into gender stereotypes. There's a reason why men and women typically do those tasks — because they are men and women. It just comes naturally. Go with it. Men and women complement each other, and together make a great team, especially when it comes to raising children. Play to your strengths.

16

Adopt this motto: Setbacks are inevitable, but failure is unthinkable.

People who get prenuptial agreements are people who get divorced. You can't go into a marriage with an exit strategy and expect the marriage to last. Take the d-word out of your vocabulary. When it comes to your marriage, that word doesn't exist. Without an easy "out," you will be more challenged to make the marriage work. So make it work.

REALIZE THAT YOUR MARRIAGE MATTERS

Your marriage matters to you, your kids, and the people around you.

17

Picture yourself five years from now. See yourself grateful that you stuck with your spouse.

Researchers from the Institute for American Values followed couples in crisis who contemplated divorce. Five years later, most of those who stayed married were glad they did. Remind yourself of this the next time you think you can't take any more. Take a deep breath, pull your shoulders back, and keep moving forward, doing what needs to be done to make things better.

18 _____

Picture yourself satisfied with life and happy to be alive, focusing on what you do have rather than what you don't.

People divorce because they believe it will make them happier. Instead of dwelling on the traits you wish your spouse had, try thinking about the positive traits that made you fall in love in the first place. Odds are that he or she hasn't changed that much.

19

Picture yourself living to a ripe old age. For men, divorce is about as dangerous as picking up a pack-a-day cigarette habit. Being unmarried shortens a woman's life span by more years than having cancer or living in poverty.

The bottom line here is clear: Your marriage matters—not just to your children and friends who need your good example, but also to yourself. If you're not trying to make it work for others' sake, can you at least do it for yourself? If your marriage is on the rocks, seek help and don't give up.

20

Imagine yourself in retirement, sitting on a pile of cash, $50,000 extra to be exact. By retirement age, the typical married couple has accumulated about $410,000 in net worth, or about $205,000 per person. By contrast, the typical divorced individual has only accumulated $154,000.

So many couples, when divorcing, squabble over who gets what, striving to get more and more from each other, as though it were a game to be won. Instead, consider how much you would have later on if you pooled your resources and stayed together. Think about how your future selves, and your children, will benefit from that accumulated wealth. Then, when you've retired, you can look back on what you've acquired and say, "We've earned it."

21

Imagine your child's graduation from high school. You're proud of her. You're proud of yourself and your spouse because you know you have contributed to your daughter's success. Children of married parents are more likely to finish high school, go to college, and have good grades than are children of divorced parents.

Sometimes divorcing couples say all they have in common anymore is the kids. As important as your children are, your spouse still comes first. Make time alone with each other a priority in order to strengthen your relationship. Then, not only will you have raised great, well-adjusted kids, but, by your example, you will help them provide you with great grandkids!

22

Imagine your child's (or future child's) wedding day. The bride is radiant. The groom is confident. They are both hopeful. Children of divorced parents have more difficulty trusting others and forming lasting relationships, and are more likely to get divorced themselves.

The foundation for happily married couples begins with happily married parents. Instead of watching the divorce rate rise, let's help young people by demonstrating a more positive trend—lifelong marriage.

23

Think about other people who are counting on you to stay married and who would be disappointed if you divorced. Your marriage is an example to others, whether you know it or not.

Your coworkers, family, and friends will look up to you for not taking the usual and seemingly inevitable path of divorce when things get rough. Rocky patches are unavoidable. How you stand up to those challenges is what counts.

24

When you are tempted to give up, recall the words of Winston Churchill when he rallied the British troops and civilians during World War II: "We shall fight on the beaches, we shall fight on the landing grounds, we shall fight in the fields and in the streets, we shall fight in the hills; we shall never surrender." You don't have to fight. You just have to persevere in love.

These words of wisdom can apply to so many areas of your life, but none as important as your marriage. If love is war, then call a truce.

CHECK YOUR EXPECTATIONS AT THE DOOR

Many people get divorced, hoping that the next relationship will be better, but second marriages have a higher divorce rate than first marriages.

25

Expect imperfection and limitations from your spouse and yourself. You can be partners in your imperfection. This positions you to work together to solve problems, instead of competing with each other or blaming each other.

You both have a unique set of strengths and weaknesses. Take advantage of those strengths by teaming up to solve problems. My husband and I make great Trivial Pursuit partners: He knows science, history, and sports; I know literature, people, and leisure. In fact, one of the criteria I was looking for in a husband was that he be good in math, as I am abysmal. Now he can playfully pick on me for multiplying six and eight wrong, and I can jab him for misusing a comma. In the end, we just smile and laugh at ourselves. Accept your spouse's weaknesses by acknowledging that you have some of your own. Stop the blame game and realize you're on the same team.

26

Expect conflict. Accept the fact that a certain amount of conflict is inevitable in any long-lasting relationship. Low-level conflict is NOT evidence that you chose the wrong person or that something is dreadfully wrong with one or both of you.

Resolve conflicts by talking through the matter at a time when both of you are well rested, well fed, and calm. Letting issues fester will only make matters worse to the point of explosion. When appropriate, seek help from your priest or a trusted friend. If it's high-level conflict, consider marriage counseling, but don't consider giving up on your relationship.

27

Listen to what your spouse is trying to tell you during a conflict. Sometimes conflict arises because one person is trying to hold the other accountable for misbehavior, bad habits, or character flaws. You'd probably rather hear about your character defects from your spouse, who loves you, than from your boss during an exit interview.

How well do you typically do on your New Year's resolutions? Did you lose ten pounds? Are you down to only one pack a day? Are you exercising eight days a week? Well why not work on something a little more internal? Park your pride in the still-cluttered garage, and listen to what your spouse has to say. You may not enjoy it at the time. But you may end up thanking him or her later.

28

Expect disappointments; some are inevitable over the course of a lifetime. The fact that something didn't turn out the way you hoped does not prove that your spouse is the wrong person for you.

There is no such thing as a perfect person. Remember that, even about the person who is perfect *for* you. Aim for realistic expectations about your spouse and yourself, and you'll learn to deal with the difficulties as they come.

29

Learn to view personal and family problems as challenges, not as crises for the marriage. If your spouse is having a problem with his or her job or parents, support your spouse, even though he or she may be no fun to be around for a while. If you are having some kind of problem, resist the urge to blame your spouse, even though he or she is the closest target.

No couple is impervious to difficulties. Bad things will happen, but don't think that they are a sign that your marriage is flawed. There is nothing special about your marriage: Every marriage faces challenges. When struggles come along, be understanding and supportive of each other. Think about how much stronger your relationship will be as a result of surmounting this obstacle.

30

Recognize that most people are thinking of themselves most of the time. Seeing this about your spouse will save you a lot of disappointment. Seeing this about yourself will help you realize what your spouse has to put up with.

How many times have you launched into the intricacies of the all-consuming project you're working on, only to take a breath and have your spouse change the subject to whatever all-consuming task he or she is working on? Then when your spouse pauses, you go back to talking about your thing, slightly annoyed that he or she changed the subject. But no matter how important and interesting you think your project is, the world still doesn't revolve around you. If anything, it revolves around the two of you as a pair. Access your inner child, go back to kindergarten, and learn how to share.

31 _____

Take the long view. Some days you are going to fuss. Some days your spouse is going to fuss. Let your spouse fuss.

You and your spouse are both perfectly happy all day, every day, right? Well, when you wake up from your dream world, accept the fact that women *and* men have mood swings. Don't take it personally. Don't let the other person's mood bring you down, either. Try to be helpful and appease the grief rather than add anything to it. One of you has to be the strong one when you're both feeling low. Take turns doing this.

32

Expect your spouse to be different from you. Because you are two unique people, you will have distinct desires and traits. Your spouse won't react the same way you react, want the things you want, or be good at the things at which you are good.

Have you ever asked your spouse the question, "Why aren't you as upset about this as I am?" Was the answer more than a shrug? Either your spouse isn't as upset because he or she just isn't, or your spouse just shows feelings differently. Either way, be thankful. One of you needs to be level-headed and calm the other down. As far as likes and talents go, watch football with him, or watch figure skating with her. Accept the fact that he can run faster than you, or that she can make more free throws than you. Together you will learn more, and together you make a great team.

TAKE ACTION TO IMPROVE YOUR MARRIAGE

Here are some concrete tasks you can do to make a difference, even if your spouse doesn't change a bit.

33

Listen twice as much as you talk. You have two ears and one mouth. Everyone appreciates an attentive listener.

Isn't this the truth? We all know this because we've been told it so many times, but were we really *listening*? This is one truth that can never be repeated too frequently, and your spouse will appreciate the renewed efforts of listening before speaking. It should also go without saying: Don't interrupt! And don't be impatient, thinking you already know what your spouse is going to say, so you say it for him or her, only faster, so as to get on with what you want to say. Never a good idea.

34

Practice saying "yes" to your spouse. If you can agree with him or her, do so.

I haven't heard of any relationships that thrive on arguing. Have you? Then don't make a point of doing it, especially not just for kicks or to feel superior. No one likes that. Imagine Mary and Joseph in their humble home together. Do you think they fought? I seriously doubt it. They probably spent their time in prayer, work, and humble service of each other and their fellow man. Strive to be more like the Holy Family.

35

Practice giving to your spouse. "I'm getting up to get a cup of coffee. Can I get something for you?"

Anticipate your spouse's needs. If you notice your spouse's cup is half empty (or half full, if you prefer), get up for more before your spouse even notices he or she is running low. It will make him or her happy and even bring delight to your own heart when you know you've done a good deed. Remember, it's those little unexpected things that carry the most weight. This was St. Thérèse of Lisieux's philosophy, and she became a doctor of the Church! Follow her little way of charity, beginning with your spouse.

36

Relinquish control of small issues. You will be building up the feeling of teamwork within your home. You will feel a lot less stressed yourself if you let go of the need to win on trivial issues. And you'll be in a much stronger position to stand your ground when the two of you disagree over something really important.

"Don't sweat the small stuff, or you'll drown in it." In a marriage it's critical to recognize the small stuff and to remember what is the biggest: your relationship. Don't raise your blood pressure because she ate the last of the mint chocolate chip ice cream or because he squeezes the toothpaste from the middle instead of the end. But really, in the little debates, the one who feels less strongly on the matter should simply give in to the other. Keep the peace, and keep your spouse.

37

Always speak well of your spouse, both in private and in public. Badmouthing your spouse to others makes you look either disloyal or foolish, or both. Say nothing if you truly can't think of anything positive to say.

Not only is this about the way you appear to other people, but it's also about how you end up relating to your spouse. If you're saying negative things about the other person behind his or her back, it will inevitably trickle into your conversations with your spouse and affect your disposition toward him or her. Nip this scenario in the bud by simply keeping your mouth shut.

38

Give your spouse the benefit of the doubt, even in your mind. If you find yourself mentally rehearsing your grudges, change the subject. Harboring negative thoughts will make you sour.

Have you ever taken a picture of someone right as they sneezed? Those pictures never turn out well. And sometimes when we talk, we say something we didn't actually mean; it didn't come out right. Sometimes we're just having an off day and speak or act more harshly than we normally would. If your spouse does something out of the ordinary, in a hurtful sort of way, he or she may just be having an off day. Give him or her some space and time, and think of that incident as the moment when he or she sneezed as the picture snapped. Throw the photo, and the incident, out of your mind.

39

Remove all forms of sarcasm from your vocabulary. The word sarcasm comes from a Greek word meaning "to tear flesh like dogs." There is never a good time or good reason to tear your spouse's flesh.

For some people, sarcasm is their primary form of expressing humor. How many times has someone lofted a mildly amusing yet cunningly biting "joke" in your direction followed by, "Just kidding"? Joke or no, it hurts. It's the same with sarcasm. If you're the type of person who enjoys this form of "banter," remember its Greek translation and keep your tongue from wagging.

GET IT DONE
WITHOUT DRAMA

End the haggling over household chores.

40

Aim for a "hundred-hundred" marriage, where each person gives 100 percent. You want to be able to say, "I do all I can for you, and you do all you can for me." A "fifty-fifty" marriage, where each person does 50 percent of everything, is for people who don't trust each other.

Real love means giving 100 percent even, and especially, when it hurts and not just when it comes to chores. This might mean letting him make the final call on the vacation arrangements, giving up a night out with the guys when she's had a rough day and just wants to relax with you, folding his socks just the way he likes even though you disagree, or letting her choose the dessert you plan on sharing. Make the decision to place your love for him or her above other things, including yourself.

41

Strive to do all you can for your spouse, even if he or she, for some reason, is unable to give you very much. You are more likely to inspire generosity by being generous yourself rather than by demanding fairness.

Lead by example. You have particular needs and so does your spouse. Sometimes that need is being pampered. Other times it's being left alone. Respect and understand your spouse's wishes. When it comes your time to be needy, trust you will be treated likewise to the best of your spouse's particular ability.

42

Give the relationship time for reciprocity to develop. People are unable to give much for a variety of reasons. Sometimes one person is sick or preoccupied. These times pass.

All things, relationships included, ebb and flow like the tides. You can't be perfect and fully on top of your game at all times, and neither can your spouse. Recognize that. Do what you can, and hope that your efforts will bear fruit.

43

Make reasonable allowances for differences in personality. Your spouse may be impatient. Don't expect him or her to be interested in helping with every tedious job in the household.

There are, no doubt, chores that your spouse does that you are so glad you don't have to do. Likewise, there are certainly some tasks that you do for which your spouse is very grateful. And then there are the jobs neither one of you wants to do. Compromise. Do them together or take turns, each of you to the best of your ability. Work it out reasonably in such a way that you are both satisfied. Or, better yet, when appropriate, make the kids do it!

44

Give extra credit to your spouse whenever you can. Your spouse may be hypersensitive to blood, gore, and sickness. If he or she stays up with a sick child, give your spouse extra credit for overcoming his or her natural disinclination to do so.

People are different, that's for sure. And it's a good thing, too. A lot of things would never get done if it were all up to me! So give your spouse credit whenever you can, especially when he or she goes the extra mile. Don't let that added effort go unnoticed and unrewarded. And when you can, go the extra mile for your spouse, too.

45

Accept the fact that each of you is good at a different set of things and cares about a different set of things.

I hate football season. I absolutely dread it every year. To make things worse, it often begins on or around my birthday. For my husband, however, it's the most wonderful time of the year. Consequently, I must endure countless monologues about quarterbacks, linebackers, conferences, stats, and other information that filters loosely through my mind while I try to figure out what to make for dinner. As much as it pains me to endure this useless information, I know that he loves to talk football, and I'm the only person around, short of an imaginary friend, who will listen even remotely. With your loved ones, you make allowances. That's just the way it is.

46

Use the Generosity Gauge, rather than the Fairness Filter. When your spouse asks you to do something, don't ask whether you owe it to him or her, or whether he or she deserves it, or what your spouse did for you lately. Ask instead, "Can I do this for him or her?"

"Don't think, just do," would be bad advice in almost any situation, but not when it comes to an honest and worthy request from your spouse. Make saying "yes" your default setting of dealing with one another. If you can do it, then do it.

RECOGNIZE THAT WINNING IS FOR LOSERS

Have fewer fights.

47

Realize that some quarrels are not over the issue at hand. Quarrels over what to have for dinner, or how to line up the socks in the drawer, are not about food or socks. These arguments are about winning.

Or quarrels are about a deeper issue that is hiding and wants to come out. If your spouse starts an all-out war because you put a fork in the dishwasher in the wrong place, it may be time to ask him or her, "What is really bothering you?" If there is some underlying turmoil and built-up resentment, it needs to be discussed openly, lovingly, and honestly before it festers any further. That old adage, "communication is key," is especially true for healthy, happy marriages. But if the issue is just about winning, know that real winners are those who give in on small things in order to keep the peace.

48

Learn to give way on trivial issues. Needing to win an unimportant argument is not a sign of strength. It is a sign of weakness.

If you find yourself fighting with your spouse just for the sake of being "right" or "winning," take a second and realize what you're trying to achieve. If you think about it, you'll realize just how silly it is. Loving your spouse comes first. Winning comes last.

49

Make sure you are not a person who must prevail in every disagreement. These people are very difficult to live with.

This one's pretty self-explanatory, and you all know the type of people I'm talking about. They're akin to know-it-alls and tend to start arguments just for the joy of it and for the sake of being right about one more thing. Don't let this happen to you! Be honest. If the other person is right, let it go and let him or her win. You may not win the argument, but you won't lose a friend or spouse!

50

Ask yourself how important the issue really is. What is the worst thing that can happen if your spouse wins this quarrel?

Be humble. Suck it up and let it go. Many times, the biggest win comes simply in surrendering first.

51 _____

Remove your self-esteem from the argument. You have a choice about how to handle not getting what you want. If your self-esteem depends on always getting your own way or always being right, your self-esteem will always be fragile.

Base your self-worth on the knowledge that you are beloved by God. Don't let a momentary exchange define who you are and how much you like yourself.

52

View disappointments in quarrels as curve balls, not as crises. If you really believe in yourself, you'll know that you can handle curve balls. Make a decision to handle them.

If the only curve ball you've been thrown is having lost the argument, just remember: winning is for losers. In a relationship, you want your spouse to be happy. If he or she is happy, you're happy. Let the other person winning the argument make you happy.

53

Remind yourself that your spouse is your life partner, not your enemy. Find a way to work together to solve the problem at hand. If the problem is important enough to deserve a solution, solving it is more important than who wins.

Life is hard enough when you don't have someone to share it with and to help you along the way. Your spouse is there for you when you're sick, when you desperately need something from the store, when you want to vent about work issues, or when you need help opening a jar. You've chosen each other for the job, and it's a lifelong position. Remember that no one else in the world loves you the way this person loves you. Why would you let something as normal as an argument ruin that? To truly love each other means wanting the best for each other. Wanting to always one-up your spouse means you love yourself more than you love him or her. Work on that.

54

Say, "Let me think about it," when your spouse comes up with an idea different from yours. This gives you time to think before you speak. You are not required to defend all your own ideas before listening to alternatives.

This might mean leaving the room for a while. Just be sure to let your spouse know that you will get back to him or her soon. Take some time to think things through before you make any rash statements that you may regret later. If you truly listen and think about the alternative idea posed by your spouse, you may realize that it is better than your own. Be happy about that.

55

Do not, under any circumstances, attack your spouse's character during the heat of an argument. Telling your spouse that he or she is a hot-headed idiot is not a good idea when you are both angry.

Who becomes the hot-headed idiot then? Name calling is immature and unhelpful. Seek higher ground.

56

Avoid absolute statements such as, "you never" or "you always."

Such statements are likely to cause additional arguments rather than resolve anything anyway. It's not loving to perpetuate a fight. Stick to the issue at hand, and above all else, be honest with yourself and kind to your spouse.

57

Avoid making comparisons, even if you think they are accurate. Statements like, "I would never do a thing like that to you," will not win you any points. Your spouse won't believe you. Besides, you are not likely to be making sound judgments when your adrenaline is flowing.

Perhaps it would be best to take that adrenaline in a different direction by going for a jog. Take advantage of the opportunity to blow off some steam and get exercise at the same time. Exercise is proven to be helpful both physically and emotionally. If a jog isn't an option, gently close the door to your room and slam out some sit-ups and/or push-ups. You'll feel better for having done so in more ways than one. Then, once you've cooled off, return to the discussion with a more level head (and slightly firmer abs).

58

Refrain from offering your spouse suggestions for his or her self-improvement during a disagreement. Most people are resistant to hearing anything negative about themselves. Your suggestions are likely to backfire, even under the best of circumstances, which the height of a quarrel certainly isn't.

You should probably start by asking yourself whether or not your suggestion really needs to be said. This decision can't be made while in a state of anger. When you are calm, ask yourself if your criticism was a result of your ire during the fight, or if it represents a legitimate need for improvement. If the latter, choose an appropriate opportunity for voicing your concern. Also, couch it in such a way that it comes off as delicately as possible, perhaps even accusing yourself as well: "You and I should probably both try to . . ."

59

Ask yourself these questions before you ask your spouse to change in some way: "Do I want him or her to change so that I can be more comfortable? Is this change really in his or her interest? Is this change even important?"

Maybe instead there are changes *you* need to make for the betterment of yourself and your relationship with your spouse. If your spouse were to ask changes of you, what do you think they would be? Can you make them even before being asked?

UNDERSTAND THE PHYSIOLOGY OF FIGHTING

*Knowing your body can reduce
your stress and help your marriage.*

60

Be aware that an argument has physiological consequences. Your body produces increased levels of stress hormones during quarrels. If you sometimes think you can feel the anger in your veins, you are absolutely right.

This means that quarrels can literally take years off your life. So learn to take responsibility for your anger. You'll help your body, and your marriage.

61

Pay attention to how you react during arguments. Researchers from Ohio State University have shown that couples who have high levels of stress hormones during a quarrel are more likely to get divorced than couples with lower levels of stress hormones. If you are a "high-stress couple" or a "high-stress person," make some plan for managing your stress level before, during, and after fights.

Exercise, a glass of wine, a bubble bath perhaps? If you are a high-stress person, why not spend some time contemplating what stresses you out so much and what can be done to rectify that. Is it your job? Perhaps it's time for a change. If it's your spouse, perhaps it's time for some counseling or a few of the aforementioned activities, preferably together. It's hard to be stressed out about your spouse while you're in a bathtub drinking wine together.

62

Make allowances for differences between you and your spouse. For instance, women tend to have higher levels of stress hormones in their systems than men the day after a quarrel. If this is true in your marriage, the woman may be battling with her own body as much as with her husband in the aftermath of a fight.

Bottom line: Men, tread softly even the day after the argument. If you're not careful, you may start the fight over again and then have to wait even longer to get things back to normal. Try not to hold it against her. It probably bugs her just as much as it does you, if not more. Women, try to remember this about your body if you find yourself still on edge the next day.

HANDLE CRITICISM GRACEFULLY

Your spouse can be a great source of insight into your own character, which means you can learn a lot about yourself by just listening.

63

Protect yourself when your spouse starts criticizing you. Imagine yourself inside a giant bell-shaped jar. You can observe what is going on around you, but the jar protects you from anything harmful actually coming in. This gives you some psychological space to begin listening.

This is an opportunity for you to learn and grow, but that can be a difficult and painful task. Pretend you are watching this encounter unfold on television. You are now the writer. How would you write this scene to provide the best possible outcome for both of you? When it's your turn to speak, be both the director and the star. You can take the high road and only accept what you think is valuable from your spouse's comments.

64

Listen to the message, not the delivery. Your spouse may be angry and nasty, but he or she still may have something to say that is true. Make an effort to look past the bulging arteries and clenched fists.

Listen carefully. Try to take yourself outside of yourself—outside of the part of you that wants to take everything to heart and react harshly. Filter everything but the underlying message out of what you are seeing and hearing at this time. Focus on that message only, and figure out what you need to do to solve the actual problem.

65

Remind yourself that you are not required to believe what your spouse says.

When things get ugly, we say lots of things we don't necessarily mean. Sometimes we say things just for the sake of blowing off steam or getting in the last word. You can probably ignore a lot of what is said in these types of situations. Let that stuff go in one ear and out the other, and try not to say those things yourself.

66

Remind yourself that it is in your best interest to know what your spouse has to say. Your spouse is telling you something about what he or she believes to be true or something about what he or she is feeling. You don't have to agree in order to absorb the fact that this is what the other person thinks or feels.

Everybody is entitled to his or her feelings. You cannot fault your spouse for feeling a certain way in a given situation. You don't have to feel the same way in order for your spouse's feelings to be valid. Understanding how your spouse feels in this scenario will be of future benefit to you both.

67

Pause. Let your spouse know that you heard what he or she said. Make a promise to your spouse and yourself to think about what the other person had to say.

A sure-fire way to shorten an argument is to take a breather and think about what was said and how to respond calmly, humbly, and fairly. Just say, "Thank you for that information. I will think it over and get back to you as soon as I can."

68

Allow yourself to have some feelings about what was said. How does it feel that your husband thinks you're a shrew? How does it feel that your wife thinks you never contribute to household chores? Remind yourself that these are just feelings, not action items. Don't trouble yourself at this moment with the question of whether you really are a shrew or you really don't do your share.

If your spouse thinks you nag too much, your first inclination is likely to think, "No, I don't!" But the fact of the matter is, your spouse still feels that you do. Take a second to ponder that. What you think you did or didn't do is not necessarily the relevant point. How your spouse feels and what you can do to help your spouse feel better, is.

69

When your spouse hurts your feelings, think about what was said. Is there any truth to your spouse's complaint? How would you feel if the roles were reversed? Can you give your spouse what he or she is asking for? It is in your best interest to be honest with yourself at this point.

Nobody enjoys looking in the metaphorical mirror and seeing the need for change. But it's your job to assess the extent of that need for yourself, not for your spouse. You cannot *make* each other change. You have to want to improve yourself, for your own good, and for the good of the relationship, which is the most important thing.

70

Be as generous as you can with your spouse. If you can, thank him or her for bringing this issue to your attention. If you can, tell your spouse you think he or she has a point. If you can, sympathize with how your spouse feels, even if you don't agree with the point he or she is making.

This may be very difficult. Try working on one step at a time and then working your way up to the trifecta. Can you imagine how quickly and easily this attitude will diffuse a potentially explosive situation? And with any luck, your spouse will catch on and follow your lead. Arguments will morph into productive relationship-building conversations in no time.

Soothe Yourself to Let Go of Grudges

If you want to stay married, you must take responsibility for your own stress level.

71

Get touched. Touch reduces stress. That's the kind of animals we humans are. So pet the dog, cuddle the cat, or hug the kids.

When you're having a difficult conversation, try having it sitting on the couch next to each other. Perhaps your arms or knees will be touching, maybe even just your feet. It's far more awkward to yell at each other when you're so physically close; plus, just the slightest bit of physical contact reduces the tension. The discussion will go much better in this situation versus standing across the kitchen from each other. Try it out sometime.

72

Ask your spouse for a hug or a touch, if he or she is ready.

I don't recommend going in guns blazing, arms wide and lips parted. Nothing is more off-putting than forced affection when it hardly seems the appropriate time. Move in slowly, taking baby steps. Doing so literally might be so cute that your spouse actually laughs. Bomb diffused; problem solved.

73

Stay in bed with each other if you've had a fight at bedtime. If you are the one lying awake, go ahead and touch your spouse. You might very well feel better, and the sleepy-head next to you won't know the difference.

If you feel comfortable enough to snuggle, the sleepy-head may notice, and may really appreciate it. Then you'll both sleep better. But, of course, feel out the situation first.

74

Pray rather than lying awake at night.

When you can't sleep because you're too busy thinking about how irritated you are with your spouse, pray. And don't just pray about *your* situation—offer some prayers for the many people you know who are having difficult times. And if you can't think of many, think about world situations that need serious intercession. This may help you calm yourself as well as put your own problems into perspective. Ask Our Lord and Our Lady to guide you.

75

Get up and do something constructive. Don't lie awake after a fight for very long. You are likely to rehearse the quarrel and every old complaint you've ever had against your spouse.

This provides a great opportunity to accomplish a task and therefore provide one positive aspect to an otherwise negative situation.

76

Break out of negative thought patterns. Do something that has nothing to do with whatever you are fighting about. You need to mentally change the subject.

Pick up a good book or magazine to divert your attention. Watch a bit of TV, or surf the net. Give yourself at least a half an hour to settle down while formulating your response to your spouse. When the time comes, you will then be better able to present your case in a calm and loving manner.

77

Be grateful if your spouse is better at changing the subject than you are. Don't put him or her down for avoiding the issue. Changing the subject may be the most constructive thing you can do at that particular moment.

At first you may be unsettled by the sudden shift in conversation. Pause, take a breath, and go with the flow. Then you can move to your separate corners for a while. Regroup when you are both ready. If you have a spouse who can diffuse the tension by cracking a joke in the midst of an argument, consider yourself lucky. You have a keeper.

78

Plan another time to discuss the issue or solve the problem you're fighting about.

Certain times just aren't good for arguments. Late at night, right before dinner when you're both hungry, or when company is over are obvious examples. "Don't go to bed angry" is not the best advice. Chances are, you won't be thinking clearly or rationally when you're tired. Sometimes, it's better to postpone the inevitable discussion so that each of you can have time to cool off and think out your position rationally. Just remember that when you do return to the war room, be honest, open, and willing to listen.

79

Do something to take care of your own needs. Particularly if you feel threatened in some way by the subject of the argument, be sure that you are taking responsibility for taking good care of your legitimate needs.

This may mean walking away. It may mean going for a drive and visiting an adoration chapel. You know what you need to do. Don't be afraid to do it when the situation warrants it.

80

Sing. We often "get stuck" on a negative idea during a fight. Neuroscience has shown that singing helps us use both halves of the brain. Singing helps you get "unstuck."

You may find yourself starting off with "These boots are made for walking," or "Any man of mine better walk the line," but after a while, you'll be able to move yourself on from the thwarted romance genre to a sappy love song, preferably a duet.

81

Take a walk or do something else physical. This interrupts your thought patterns and reduces your stress level.

Rotate the tires or defrost the freezer if need be. You'll get some exercise and accomplish a dreaded task while you cool off. Win-win!

82

Cultivate an attitude of gratitude. Remind yourself of something good your spouse has done for you.

Think back to the joys of dating, the euphoria of getting engaged, the magic of your wedding day. "How do I love thee, let me count the ways" shouldn't be too difficult. You married each other for many good reasons. When the going gets tough, remind yourself of those reasons.

ASK FOR HELP WITHOUT WHINING, COMPLAINING, OR DEMANDING

You don't have to do everything yourself if you know how to ask for help. Allow your spouse to give to you. Allow yourself to be a little bit dependent.

83

Say simply, "This task is important to me. Would you be willing to help me?"

Everybody likes being useful and needed. Plus, it's far easier to respond positively to a request when it is made rationally, without whining and complaining.

84

Make a simple request for information. "I don't quite see how to do this myself. Do you have any ideas?"

This method will likely get you much better results than saying, "Do this for me." That would fall under the category of demanding, and is not nearly so nice as asking.

85

Ask for help in a straightforward way: "I am really tired, but I would like to see this job completed. Would you be willing to help me?"

Memorize that phrase! Think about how much more effective it is than, "Why aren't you helping me?! Can't you see that I'm tired? You're not doing anything anyway!" Which approach do you think will produce the desired effect?

86

Avoid statements like "I did all the laundry. You owe it to me to do the dishes." These comparisons sound manipulative and invite retaliation, as in, "Well, I took out the garbage, and you didn't." There is no end to that sort of thing. Give it up.

Do what you do and let your spouse do what he or she does. There are no score cards when it comes to having a happy marriage. Each of you needs to do your part without complaint to keep things running along smoothly.

OFFER HELP WITHOUT BEING DEMEANING

Loving people help others to solve problems. Busybodies push people aside to show them the One True Way to Do It.

87 _____

Offer to help by saying, "May I assist you?" Don't grab the job out of the other person's hands.

If you do confiscate someone else's duty, you irritate and/or humiliate that person. Also, your spouse then might say, "Well, fine then. If you want to do it, you can do it from now on." If you're going to be grabby, be sure it's at least for a task you're willing to make your own.

88

Extend yourself in an open-ended way, as in, "How can I help?" If you just blunder ahead and solve the problem, your spouse may feel you don't respect his or her ability to solve it.

Plus, you'll take away the satisfaction your spouse will receive from having solved the issue on his or her own. The self-confidence gained in a situation such as this may be a necessary tool in completing larger, more difficult tasks. Allow your spouse this opportunity to grow.

89

Volunteer to listen to the other person's needs, as in, "What would be helpful to you?" This gives your spouse an opportunity to let you know what he or she really needs. You may be completely mistaken.

Wouldn't it be funny if your spouse said he or she wanted ham and cheese, but you heard, and therefore made, peanut butter and jelly? This could be an occasion for a good laugh, or, in a more serious situation, it could cause lasting marital strife. Make sure you get it right and avoid the possibility of disaster.

90

Volunteer information in a way that allows the other person to refuse. "You might try doing it this way. I had good luck with that once. Can I show you?"

Consider the alternative approach: stamping your foot, sighing heavily, muttering "you idiot" under your breath. Which would you rather hear from your spouse? And if the first approach doesn't work, walk away and leave the person alone. Perhaps your spouse works better without an audience. And if your attempts to help are harshly spurned, chalk it up to the frustration of the moment, and let it go.

MAKE FORGIVENESS MORE IMPORTANT THAN SEX

People often forget a great sexual encounter five minutes after it is over. But they will remember their grudges for a lifetime.

91

Say, "I am sorry I hurt you." This can be hard to say, but it won't kill you.

Honesty is the best policy. If you mess up, fess up. It speaks volumes about your character and maturity.

92

Admit you were wrong. Owning up to your own imperfection allows you to be human. Your spouse has an opportunity to forgive you and to connect with you as one frail, fragile, imperfect, blundering human being to another.

Remember Adam and Eve, apple, snake, that whole bit? Yeah, they kind of blew it for the rest of us, but we forgive them, knowing we probably would have made the same mistake. Their first sin of pride makes it difficult for us to fight our own pride. But if Adam and Eve can forgive each other for getting themselves kicked out of the equivalent of San Diego, for say, Detroit, then we can humble ourselves and forgive each other for our small transgressions. The fate of the world, aka your marriage, may depend on it.

93

Confess, "I didn't mean to hurt you. I didn't realize this would bother you so much." Don't try to fake it. Only say this if it is true.

You may have read the beginning of this tip thinking, "Sure, no problem. I can do that." Then when you got to the "only say it if it's true" part you thought, "Oh. Dang." You won't have to fake it if you strive to not do anything that would potentially hurt your spouse in the first place. What a revolutionary idea! Then if you inadvertently hurt your spouse, you can honestly say, "I'm sorry. I didn't mean to hurt you."

94

Confess even more: "I did mean to hurt you. I was angry. My feelings were hurt. I wanted to get back at you. I was wrong to try to hurt you. I hope you can forgive me."

I know; this is a tough one. But if it is true, and you can learn to say it, believe me, you will greatly improve the quality of your life and your marriage.

95

Be gracious when your spouse apologizes to you. "Thank you for your apology. I really appreciate you saying that to me."

Doesn't that come off even nicer than "Apology accepted"? And especially more than "See, I told you I was right!" Get in the habit of accepting others' defeat graciously, as well as your own!

96

Give your spouse a bit of information to make it real that you heard him or her. "I accept your apology. It was awful for me when you said what you said."

It would probably be good to follow this with, "And I realize it was a little harsh when I said 'such and such.' I apologize if I stepped over the line a bit, too." It's good form to make amends for any damage you may have done yourself. It will certainly help smooth things over and have you both feeling better that much sooner.

97

Keep your spouse in the loop if you are still hurt and need more time. "I am not quite ready to forgive you. Thank you for apologizing. Give me a little more time, please."

Imagine your spouse's reaction to that phrase. Now imagine how he or she would react if you instead shouted, "Yeah, well, that's not good enough! I'm still mad!" You'd be lucky if your spouse didn't take back his or her apology and renew the argument with some shouting of his or her own.

APPRECIATE YOUR SPOUSE

You can accomplish a great deal in life if you are willing to let other people share the credit. Gratitude is the best antidote for self-pity.

98

Notice the small things your spouse does. Express gratitude freely and frequently. It greases the wheels of the family.

Undoubtedly, there are a myriad of little things you do that unintentionally irritate your spouse. They may be too minor for your spouse to mention, but they still add up. A compliment or an unexpected simple thank you counts ten times more, and will go far to erase the memory of prior annoyances.

99

Be ready for your spouse to be suspicious of you at first. If you have a history of quarreling over household chores, your spouse will think you are thanking him or her in order to get something. Accept the other person's suspicion and thank him or her anyway.

Just take the high road. No need to give further explanation for your behavior. Eventually your sincerity will become evident.

100

Practice these phrases until they roll off your tongue: "I really appreciate you doing that for me." "Thank you." "This is really helpful to me. I could not do this without your help." "You do so much for our family. I am grateful to you."

And "I'm grateful *for* you." All those phrases will go a long way, and you know it. So don't hesitate; start using them! Perhaps it will sound a little wooden at first. Practice in front of a mirror if you have to. Eventually you'll be able to do it without even thinking, and your spouse, and you, will be all the happier for it!

101

Allow yourself to enjoy your spouse's surprises. He or she contributes to your household in all sorts of ways that might never occur to you. "I did not think of playing games with the children. I was focused on chores, and you created some pleasure in our home. Thank you."

It's good every once in a while to do something spontaneous. It keeps the marriage fresh and lively. Be happy to receive such actions and open to doing them yourself. Pay attention, also, to the nonspontaneous but wonderful things your spouse does all the time that you may take for granted. The example in the aforementioned tip also reminds us to occasionally take a break from the daily grind and to appreciate what really matters: your faith, your spouse, and your family. Enjoy them!

CONCLUSION

There you have it. One hundred and one ways to make your marriage last, complete with practical applications! Now there's just one last thing to remember: The best tip, which we have saved for last, is simply this: Pray every day for your marriage. The Sacrament of Marriage gives you the grace you need to keep the love alive, but asking for assistance daily certainly helps. Remember that a marriage is made of three people: husband, wife, and God. Never forget the "silent partner!" May God bless you and your marriage!

Jennifer Roback Morse, a renowned marriage and family scholar, is the founder and president of the Ruth Institute—a project of the National Organization for Marriage Education Fund. She is the author of two books on marriage and economics and her numerous academic and public policy articles appear in such publications as *Journal of Economic History, Forbes, Harvard Journal of Law and Public Police, and National Review Online*. She and her husband are the parents of one birth child and one adopted child. They live in San Diego, California.

Betsy Kerekes is the author of the popular blog *Parenting is Funny*. Her professional experience includes journalism and public relations for Franciscan University of Steubenville, where she graduated *summa cum laude* in writing, with a minor in communications. She also did proofreading and subscriptions management for Patrick Madrid's *Envoy* magazine, and now writes weekly newsletters and manages a blog for the Ruth Institute. Kerekes is also the editor and compiler of a desk calendar titled "365 Ways to Enjoy Your Marriage More." She telecommutes from her home near San Diego, where she homeschools her three children.